THE PIANO SONORITY OF
CLAUDE DEBUSSY

Claude Debussy. Portrait at Eragny, 1902.

THE PIANO SONORITY OF CLAUDE DEBUSSY

Virginia Raad

Studies in the History and Interpretation of Music
Volume 43

The Edwin Mellen Press
Lewiston/Queenston/Lampeter

Library of Congress Cataloging-in-Publication Data

Raad, Virginia.
　　The piano sonority of Claude Debussy / Virginia Raad.
　　　　p.　　cm. -- (Studies in the history and interpretation of music
　; v. 43)
　　　Includes bibliographical references.
　　　ISBN 0-7734-9138-4
　　　1. Debussy, Claude, 1862-1918. Piano music.　2. Piano music-
-Analysis, appreciation.　3. Performance practice (Music)-
-France--20th century.　I. Title.　II. Series.
MT145.D4R3　　1993
786.2'092--dc20　　　　　　　　　　　　　　　　　93-50847
　　　　　　　　　　　　　　　　　　　　　　　　　　　　CIP
　　　　　　　　　　　　　　　　　　　　　　　　　　　　MN

This is volume 43 in the continuing series
Studies in the History and Interpretation of Music
Volume 43 ISBN 0-7734-9138-4
SHIM Series ISBN 0-88946-426-X

A CIP catalog record for this book is available from the British Library.

The Edwin Mellen Press　　　　　　　The Edwin Mellen Press
Box 450　　　　　　　　　　　　　　　　　Box 67
Lewiston, New York　　　　　　　　　　Queenston, Ontario
USA　14092-0450　　　　　　　　　　　CANADA　L0S 1L0

The Edwin Mellen Press, Ltd.
Lampeter, Dyfed, Wales
UNITED KINGDOM　SA48 7DY

Printed in the United States of America

I dedicate this volume to Homer Ulrich (deceased) who originally edited a portion of this work over a period of several years for *The American Music Teacher*.

CONTENTS

ILLUSTRATIONS

PREFACE

It has been my intent to write on the one aspect of Debussy's piano music which is unique. Others have reviewed his life and composition extensively. However, it is as a pianist that I have found Debussy particularly interesting for he used his instrument as no other composer.

In the early work, there are glimpses of sonorous exploration. However, essentially, there are still the scale passages, arpeggios, chords, etc. of an earlier generation. As Debussy's work developed, the traditional technique of a pianist was not used for the passage in itself, but to evoke atmospheric color. The form tightened, harmonies became more obscure and rhythm became either more elastic or quite definitive depending on the subject he evoked. The touch of the pianist was to create the sonority of fog, cathedral bells or the strum of the guitar.

Though Debussy's mature work was to appear some years after the exhibition of the Anonymous Society of Painters, Sculptors and Engravers -- a group that came to be known as the Impressionists, he joined them in their essential aesthetic which was to capture the luminescence that would evoke an atmosphere.

ACKNOWLEDGEMENTS

I wish to acknowledge the countless students and faculty in the colleges and universities which I have visited throughout America. Their interest in my informal concerts, lectures and master classes at which I often play and discuss the work of Claude Debussy has always been a challenge.

Mademoiselle Berthe Bert, piano teacher at the Ecole Normale de Musique, Paris, who knew Debussy, first established my interest in his music. Professor Emile Damais of the Ecole Normale supervised my first thesis on the piano music of Claude Debussy. My doctoral dissertation at the Sorbonne, which investigated the folk elements in Debussy's work, was prepared under the supervision of Professor Jacques Chailley. He hosted the international Debussy centennial celebration at the University of Paris at which I was a participant.

Madame Gaston de Tinan, stepdaughter of the composer, shared many memories with me from my student days until her death. Oswald d'Estrade-Guerra, Debussy scholar and pupil of Ricardo Viñes, the performer who introduced Debussy's piano work, encouraged my interpretation of the composer's music. To these splendid individuals, I am indebted.

PART I

CLAUDE DEBUSSY, PIANIST

Claude Debussy's instrument was the piano. His formal training began at the age of ten when he entered the piano class of Antoine Marmontel at the Paris Conservatoire in October, 1872.

Camille Bellaigue described his fellow student:

> "At last, my child, you are here!" said Marmontel as he saw a puny little fellow entering late. Dressed in a belted blouse, the tardy boy held in his hand a kind of beret with a border and a tassle like a sailor's cap. Nothing about him, his appearance, his conversation or his playing, suggested an artist. The only remarkable thing about his face was his forehead. He was one of the youngest pianists and not one of the best. I especially remember his habit of marking the beat by a kind of hiccup or harsh breath. This rhythmic exaggeration later was to be the least of his faults. You will agree when you know his name: Claude Debussy.[1]

Bellaigue further noted that the piano class of Marmontel was held in a sparsely furnished room which had a few benches and a large Erard grand. Each student took his turn before Marmontel, a little man with a shaved head whose fingers seemed worn by the exercise of his art. About sixty, at the time of Bellaigue's encounter, he had an unmatched reputation and resembled a patriarch of the piano. Each student worked individually then played his particular work. Therefore, there was a variety of observations and advice. Bellaigue said:

> Nothing escaped Marmontel, not our manner of execution, a fault in fingering or our poor taste. Yet he never admonished us or had us repeat; all of this with kindness, even with a seeming unconcern. He was sensitive, perceptive. Sometimes, he seized his long beard in both hands and pulled it as though to lengthen it even more; with his eyes half-closed, he sighed deeply and murmured: "Oh! mon dieu! Oh! mon dieu!" One could say that he sought heaven as his witness to our blunders and the suffering he was caused.[2]

Another member of Marmontel's class, Paul Vidal, described a Debussy he knew in October 1878:

> Debussy made an immediate impression on me by his particular air with his black curly hair brought down on his forehead, his ardent gaze and his contained fierce appearance; there was something savage about him. I won him over and we quickly became good friends.

> Debussy, who had obtained the second prize in piano, two years earlier, hoped to win the first at the end of 1879, but he failed, which was for him, and certainly for his family, who hoped to see him have a brilliant career as a pianist, a large disappointment.[3]

> His playing, though very interesting, was not entirely pianistic; he had difficulty with the trill, on the other hand he had a very agile left hand which was capable of extraordinary extensions.

> His gifts as a pianist were apparent most of all in Bazille's Accompaniment Class the following years where he distinguished himself.[4]

Enrolled in Bazille's class the year of 1879-1880, Debussy won a first prize. Bazille, himself, noted in Debussy's examination notes that he could work better, but that he had great facility, good fingers, was a harmonist and something of a fantasist.

The latter quality was evident one spring morning in 1884 at the Conservatoire. Maurice Emmanuel recalled:

> A few days before the Prix of Rome, Delibes had asked his assistant to replace him. Because of a misunderstanding, neither man came to our class. After a wait, we were going to leave the somber classroom...when the door half-opened and a tossled head peered in and looked us over. The individual entered: "Dear orphans," he exclaimed, "in the absence of your superiors, I will teach you!" And he seated himself at the piano.
>
> I can tell you that it wasn't Claude Achille who mystified us that day, but the man he was to become. He sounded an array of chords which, despite their irregularities, we couldn't help but admire; [they were] blissful. There was a shimmering of odd arpeggios, a rumbling of three-note trills in both hands at once, a series of indefinable harmonies -- even if one referred to a sacred treatise, which threw us into a tumult. For more than an hour, breathless, we encircled the piano before which quivered the curly-headed mop of one possessed of the devil as the watchman, Ternusse, was to say. Alarmed by the tumult, this terrible man detected some mischief and brought the "lesson" to an end with a brusque invasion.5

Other commentaries reveal Debussy's unique personality.

After a concert on January 16, 1876, at Chauncy, where he accompanied Léontine Mendès, a singer from the Conservatoire, Samary, a cellist from the Opera and the violinist, Mansard, a reviewer noted:

> M. de Bussy, accompanist of Mlle. Mendès, is a young pianist who is in strong possession of his art. The impression of the public in regard to this young artist, before which opens a brilliant career, was that he was excellent. It seems that this child, M. de Bussy, is only 14 years old . . . [6]

In another review of the same evening:

> Mlle Mendès and M. Samary will come again to Chauncy . . . De Bussy surely will come, De Bussy who carries so much courage within his small frame. What verve! What spirit! What elan! One can no longer say that the piano is a cold instrument...this budding Mozart is a real devil. When he is at the piano, he commends his whole spirit.[7]

During the years at the Conservatoire, Debussy performed in many ways as a pianist. Marmontel recommended him, at 17, for a few months employment playing to sleep the mistress of the historic Château of Chenonceaux, Madame Marguerite Wilson-Pelouze, who suffered from insomnia. The chateau was a gathering place for artists and intellectuals. Madame Wilson-Pelouze was an active Wagnerian. The next summer, Marmontel recommended Debussy to the celebrated Madame Nadezhda von Meck, who had written to the Conservatoire and asked for a young pianist to go on a voyage with her. For three summers Debussy became a part of the von Meck entourage, journeying across Europe and Russia. Debussy, who was called *petit pianiste Bussy,* played piano duets with the mother, accompanied the daughter, Julia--an amateur singer--gave piano lessons to Sonia, theory lessons to Alexander and played in a trio with the violinist Ladislas Puchulsky and the cellist Peter Danilchenko. Madame von Meck thought that Debussy played well and that he had a brilliant technique but he lacked sensitivity. However, in her correspondence with Tchaikovsky, she commented that he sight-read magnificently.[8]

Madame Nadezhda von Meck's trio: Vladislav Pukhulsky violinist, Peter Danilchenko cellist and Debussy. Italy 1880.

Paul Vidal recommended that Debussy succeed him as an accompanist of the choral society, La Concordia. Debussy also accompanied the singing pupils of Madame Moreau-Sainti.

Marguerite Vasnier, the daughter of Blanche Adélaide Vasnier, the amateur singer whom Debussy met when accompanying the pupils of Madame Moreau-Sainti and for whom many of his early songs were created, evokes a telling portrait of Debussy:

> He wasn't happy with his family, a pretentious, not too-intelligent father, a mother whose ideas were narrow and paltry. Seldom encouraged, not supported or understood, he asked my parents if he could work at their home and from that day the door was open to him as though he were a child of the house.
>
> In an image that is both distant and a little forgotten, I can see him in a little room on the fifth floor of the rue Constantinople, where he composed most of the time during those five years. He came almost every evening, often also in the afternoon, leaving pages which he had begun on a little table.
>
> He composed at the piano, an old bizarre Blondel, which I still have. At other times, he composed as he walked. He improvised a long time, then walked all about the place singing with the constant stub of a cigarette in his mouth or rolling between his fingers paper and tobacco; then when he had discovered what he wanted, he wrote. He rewrote very little, but he searched a long time in his thoughts and at the piano before writing; moreover, he was not satisfied with his work....
>
> In the evening, my mother sang and he accompanied her; often they were happy with the music which they studied together....[9]

Debussy gave Marguerite Vasnier piano lessons. Frequently short of funds, the piano lesson was a convenient resource. He gave a lesson to pay for a modest wedding breakfast the day of his wedding to Rosalie Texier. Raoul Bardac was Debussy's student before his mother became Debussy's second wife.

Louis Laloy, friend and biographer, remarked that when Debussy lived at the rue Cardinet the most beautiful ornament in the modest apartment was an upright piano.[10] The house of Pleyel loaned Debussy an instrument during this early period. In his later years, he was to work on an upright Bechstein and a Gaveau. He also owned a Bleuthner.

For Debussy, the piano was a natural means of expression. He sometimes introduced his own works as exemplified at the Société Nationale Indépendante, May 25, 1910, when he introduced the preludes, "Danseuses de Delphes," "Voiles," "La Cathédrale Engloutie" and "La Danse de Puck." Later in the year, on December 5, 1910, he took part, with Rose Féart and the Waldbauer Quartet, in a chamber music concert in Budapest, where he played his *Estampes* and the *Childern's Corner* in a program which included his String Quartet and *Proses Lyriques.*

Debussy remarked to his friend, André Caplet, in a letter written before his voyage:

> I am going to leave in a few days for Vienna and Budapest, at last to play orchestra in one place and piano in the other. To tell you that my joy is unmixed would be a lie...I am lacking the necessary qualities for such an apostolate; in addition, since this concerns my music, it becomes almost a physical suffering![11]

Later Debussy remarked to Caplet:

> One played also at this "Gala Debussy" your arrangement for two pianos of "Iberia." Why weren't you there, you know well that I never stopped missing you. At each sonority which I knew so well, I encountered some obstacle!...And those tremolos which could arouse deaf stones! Certainly, old Caplet, music is a closed art Sunday and weekdays for too many people who go by the title "musician"! However, we stop talking...and to forget all of these galas, how I would like to hide myself in some small corner of a farm in your Normandie to hear only the songs *a capella* of the little chickens, the ironic scherzo of the sceptic ducks.[12]

Louis Laloy (1874-1944). Debussy's intimate friend and one of his first biographers. Founder of the *Mercure musical*, Secretary-General of the Opera and music critic of the *Revue des deux mondes*, he was an authority on Chinese music.

Debussy and André Caplet (1875-1925). A close friend from 1907, this composer and conductor orchestrated several of Debussy's work, even completed others.

Debussy and Stravinsky in the former's study, 1911. Era of the *Préludes*, 2e livre.

Debussy had played the transcription of "Iberia" with his friend, the celebrated pianist, Ricardo Viñes, at the Comédie des Champs-Elysées on Thursday, June 19,1913. At the same time, he introduced three more of his preludes, "Canope," "La Terrasse des Audiences au Clair de Lune" and "Hommage à S. Pickwick, Esq., P.P.M.P.C."

Debussy accompanied Mary Garden when she recorded fragments of his work, "La Chanson de Melisande" and the *Ariettes Oubliées*: "Il Pleure dans Mon Coeur," "L'Ombre des Arbres" and "Green." He, himself, recorded a number of his piano works, including several of the preludes and the *Children's Corner*. He played the Grieg Violin and Piano Sonata with Arthur Hartman and was the pianist in the Crickboom Quartet which introduced the Quartet of Lekeu, the Belgian composer. One can see Debussy informally seizing the piano to play the last act of *Pelléas* for his friend, Robert Godet, or the first act of Wagner's *Parsifal* for Ernest Chausson. A touching vignette is described by Louis Laloy:

> In the spring of 1913, on a clear afternoon, I took a few steps in my Bellevue garden with Debussy: We awaited Stravinsky. From the moment he saw us, the Russian musician ran, arms extended to give an accolade to the French master, who while waiting gave me an amused look over his shoulder. Stravinsky brought with him a piano duet arrangement of his new work, *Le Sacre du Printemps*. Debussy consented to play the bass on the Pleyel piano which I still possess. Stravinsky asked permission to remove his collar. His gaze impassive behind glasses, tippling his nose near the keyboard, at times humming a part he had cut out, he transported, in a flood of sonority the agile and soft hands of his companion who followed without trouble and seemed to make light of the difficulty. When they were finished, it was not a question of embraces nor of compliments. We were silent, crushed as after a storm...13

Later Debussy was to remark:

> Don't fall to the ground, Dear Friend, it is only me!!! Of course, if we begin, you wishing to understand and I to explain why I haven't written yet, our hair will fall out.

And then, something marvelous is happening here: at least once a day everyone talks about you. Your friend, Chouchou [Debussy's daughter, Claude-Emma, who died one year after her father], has composed a fantasy on *Petroushka* which would make tigers roar...I have threatened her with torture, but she goes on, insisting that you will "find it very beautiful." So, how could you suppose that we are not thinking of you?

Our reading at the piano of *Le Sacre du Printemps*, at Laloy's house, is always present in my mind. It haunts me like a beautiful nightmare and I try, in vain, to reinvoke the terrific impression.[14]

Stravinsky remembered:

What most impressed me at the time and what is still more memorable from the occasion of the sight-reading of *Le Sacre du Printemps* was Debussy's brilliant piano playing. Recently, while listening to his *En blanc et noir* (one of which pieces is dedicated to me) I was struck by the way in which the extraordinary quality of this pianism had directed the thought of Debussy the composer.[15]

Among Debussy's last performances was one on December 21, 1916 in which he introduced *En blanc et noir* for two pianos with Roger-Ducasse. He also accompanied Rose Féart in the *Chansons de Bilitis*, *Le Promenoir des deux amants* and "Noël des enfants qui n'ont plus de maison." On May 5, 1917, he played with Gaston Poulet the first public performance of his Sonata for Violin and Piano in a final Paris concert. André Suarès described his appearance that spring:

Debussy participated in a charity concert at which his works were played. The war which had implanted itself on his Ile-de-France showed him to be passionately French. He was terribly ill. Just a little later, he fell into his last illness. I was struck not by just his thinness or his terrible appearance but by his almost absent air and his severe lassitude. He was the color of molten wax, of ashes. His eyes weren't fevered but deep pools. There was no bitterness in his mysterious smile; he had passed the weariness of suffering. His hand was round, supple, plump, not too strong, episcopal; it weighed down his arm, his arm pulled down his shoulder, his head hung from his body, this head the seat of his unique, wonderful and cruel life...

In his eyes, which fled encounters, I saw the desperate irony which is so natural in one who is leaving life to those behind. In them were the depths of hell. On this day, one could suppose that Debussy was making his *Adieux*. He knew that he would never play again in public with those magic hands. Interpreting his own works, he never touched a strange instrument of ebony and ivory; rather, he enchanted. The play of Debussy was an incantation, the most immaterial music, with the greatest nuances one has ever heard. He didn't realize sonority as a pianist, never as a musician, but as a poet.[16]

Louis Laloy said that Debussy loved the music of Chopin, studying briefly, before the Conservatoire, with Madame Antoinette Mauté de Fleurville who may have been a pupil of Chopin. Laloy remarked:

Debussy made me understand the poetry of Chopin's music of which so many virtuosos make an exercise of the difficulty. But it is necessary, in order to see the beauty of the line, to have a lightness in tracing the lines which is not at the disposition of ordinary pianists. Even though he hadn't worked for a long time, Debussy kept the delicate touch, the suppleness of fingers, the agile hands, which seemed to shape the rapid tones and allowed one to hear without shock a pool of fluid transparency.[17]

Laloy commented in his biography that though Debussy never surpassed the second prize at the Conservatoire, he learned afterwards a "supple and alive playing, always with the fingers on the keyboard, touching, feeling the sound..."[18]

14

FOOTNOTES

1. Camille Bellaique, *Souvenirs de Music et de Musicians*, Paris, Nouvelle Librairie Nationale, 1921, p.35.

2. Ibid., p. 36.

3. Debussy won a second prize in piano, July 1877. He played the Schumann *G Minor Sonata*.

4. Paul Vidal, "Souvenirs d'Achille Debussy," *La Revue Musicale*, 1er Mai, 1926, pp. 11-12.

5. Maurice Emmanuel, "Les Ambitions de Claude-Achille," *La Revue Musicale*, 1er Mai, 1926, p. 45.

6. Henri Borgaud, "Notes et Documents," *Revue de Musicologie*, Juillet-Décembre, 1962, p. 97.

7. _____. Op. cit.

8. Edward Lockspeiser, *Debussy*, London, Dent, 1936, p. 12.

9. Marguerite Vasnier, "Debussy à dix-huit ans," *La Revue Musicale*, 1er Mai, 1926, pp 17-19.

10. Louis Laloy, *Claude Debussy*, Paris, Aux armes de France, 1944, p. 86.

11. *Lettres inédites à André Caplet*, ed., Edward Lockspeiser, Monaco, Editions du Rocher, 1957, 21 Novembre, 1910.

12. Ibid., 23 Juin 1913.

13. Louis Laloy, *La Musique Retrouvée*, Paris, Plon, 1928, p. 213.

14. Igor Stravinsky and Robert Craft, *Conversations with Igor Stravinsky*, London, Faber and Faber, 1959, pp. 49-50.

15. Ibid., p. 50.

16. André Suarès, *Debussy*, Paris, Emile-Paul, 1936, pp. 171-172, 174.

17. *La Musique Retrouvée*, pp. 122-123.

18. *Claude Debussy*, p. 2.

Debussy playing probably for the first time the score of Moussorgsky's *Boris Godounov* at the home of his close friend and benefactor Ernest Chausson, in 1893. Chausson with Etienne Dupin, financier and Debussy's faithful friend, underwrote the *Cinq Poèmes de Baudelaire* and *La Damoiselle élue*. Pictured left to right: Mme. Henri Lerolle seated, in black, Raymond Bonheur, friend and former pupil at the Conservatoire, Henri Lerolle, painter and friend of Debussy, also the brother-in-law of Chausson, who is turning pages and Mme. Chausson, in white, on the couch.

Debussy in 1898.

Jacques Durand (1865-1928). Debussy's publisher and close friend. Debussy's *Lettres à son éditeur* (Paris, A. Durand et fils, 1927) is a valuable source of information.

Debussy playing piano duets with Madame Ernest Chausson. Luzancy, 1893.

Claude Debussy in 1898. Jacques Durand said that his work table was encumbered with Japanese objects. His favorite, a toad in porcelain, was a fetish that he took everywhere saying he could not work without it. Durand also remembered that winter and summer the composer's study was filled with flowers. (*Quelques Souvenirs*, 2e séries, Paris, A. Durand et fils, 1925, p. 91.)

Ricardo Viñes (1875-1943). Spanish pianist who introduced a large part of the repertoire of Debussy and Maurice Ravel. Viñes' manner of playing was based on the complex use of two pedals. He was said to stroke the keys in such a way that he produced an unusually evocative tone. (Edward Lockspeiser, *Debussy, His Life and Mind*, Vol. II, pp. 34-35, N.Y., MacMillan, 1965.)

Antoinette-Flore Mauté (1823-1883) may have been a pupil of Chopin and apparently was an early teacher of Debussy. She was the mother of Mathilde, the forsaken wife of Verlaine.

PART II

THE EARLY WORK

The piano music that Claude Debussy composed evolved in part from his own unique keyboard performance. It reflects Debussy's preoccupation with the sonorous possibilities of his instrument which was at one time or another a Pleyel, Gaveau, Bleuthner or Bechstein. Familiar with both the upright and grand, Debussy knew essentially a nineteenth-century instrument, probably more brilliant than contemporary models, yet capable of sustained repetition and fluid translucent movement because of the double escapement modification patented earlier in the century.

Debussy knew a piano with only two pedals. It was in regard to the use of the pedal that he made one of his rare remarks about piano performance. He said to his editor, Jacques Durand:

> It is unfortunate that Madame Mauté de Fleurville, to whom I owe the little I know of the piano, is dead. She knew so much about Chopin.[1]

Debussy continued:

> I remember quite precisely what Madame Mauté de Fleurville told me. Chopin wanted one to study without the pedal, and except on certain occasions as during performance, one does not hold it. There is however the art of using the pedal as a kind of breathing, which I noted in Liszt when he played for me in Rome.
>
> The undisturbed truth is perhaps that the abuse of the pedal is but a way of concealing a lack of technique, and then it is necessary to make a lot of noise to keep one from hearing the butchered music. Theoretically, it is necessary to find a graphic means of indicating this 'respiration'...this isn't possible...[2]

During the same year, Debussy remarked to Durand:

> You know my opinion on metronomic movements: permissible for a measure...[3]

In the early works, the nineteenth century nomenclature, "Ballade," "Nocturne," "Valse romantique," "Fantaisie," is evident. There are melodies supported by mounting arpeggios, broken chords and scale-like passages, entwining "Arabesques," repetitious interval patterns which serve as pedals or become bridge passages and cadences mounting rapidly from bass to treble. Pianistic passages abound, whether in the instrumental works or in the accompaniment for the songs. In the latter, at times, the piano seems to be the solo instrument with a vocal obbligato. However, in the immature work with its traditional pianism and occasional glimpses of Fauré, Massenet, etc., there are already brief passages wherein the composer explored instrumental sonority.

The So-Called Transparent Legato

Laloy wrote of Debussy's delicate touch, supple fingers and agile hands which allowed one to hear a fluid transparency. A so-called transparent piano legato occurs in Debussy's mature works when chords supporting a motif or a melody appear in a series that can be sinuous in line. The harmonic intervals are often wide-spaced and in parallel movement. The passages are supported by harmonic and piano pedals. Sometimes Debussy's legato style appears in a pattern of notes in sequential movement with the sparkling expressiveness reminiscent of early keyboard writing. The passages require not only finger dexterity, but the sure knowledge of where the key can be restruck before returning to the original position so that the tones will not be shocking.

In the piano composition "Sarabande" (1896), there is a sinuous primary theme with wide-spaced intervals which Debussy indicated should be played "avec une élégance grave et lente." (example 1)

Example 1

The theme introduces a composition replete with parallel fourths and fifths, motifs over sonorous bass pedals and chords reproduced on different degrees of the scale.[4]

Stylistically, the "Sarabande" is related to two later *Images*, "Hommage à Rameau" (1905) and "Et la lune descend sur le temple qui fut [And the Moon Descends over the Ruin]" (1907-08). It is the second composition in a three-part suite *Pour le piano* [For the Piano] (1896-1901) of which the first is a "Prélude" and the third, a "Toccata." The last two compositions cited are animated rhythmic studies which explore the nature of an instrument capable of brilliant sound if the hammer is struck quickly. Debussy was preoccupied with the idea of movement - he even gave one of the *Images* the title "Mouvement" (1905). In works such as the "Prélude" and "Toccata" the movement is through arpeggios, scale-like passages and repetitive interval patterns which seem endless. Later Debussy frequently did not require the participation of all five fingers and created small conjunct patterns which lay under the middle fingers of the hand (i.e. "Mouvement," "Feux d'artifice [Fireworks]," "Pour les huit doigts [For the Eight Fingers].")

The Use of Piano Sonority to Evoke Other Instruments

In the early works, Debussy began to use piano sonority to suggest other instruments. In the final cadenza of the "Prélude," Debussy evoked the harp with characteristic sweeps of diatonic, glissando-like passages alternating with the whole tone scale, legato alternating with staccato simulating plucking and terraced dynamics beginning forte and diminishing to mezzo piano.

An attempt to portray the ancient pan pipe is made in the primary melodic pattern of "La Flûte de Pan" (*Chansons de Bilitis*, 1897-98). The fluid legato piano passage mounts briefly in pitch and dynamics and descends in the pentatonic mode. (example 2)

Example 2

However, it was the bell tone, largely a poetic sound, which was later to become a strong element in Debussy's mature style. The piano is capable of various legato touches and bell tones are virtuoso colors requiring perfect control of the finger and hand. The key must be struck not only rapidly but by fingers that are sensitively taut in order to exact different dynamic levels. In the immature work, the examples are rudimentary. The song "Les Cloches [The Bells]" (*Deux Romances*, 1891) has a piano motif from the folk song "Carillon du Vendôme" which rings resonantly when the pattern is repeated in the treble. Debussy explored the upper register of the piano and various pianissimo tones which are "bell-like" in the coda of the "Ballade" (1890) and in the recapitulation of the "Clair de lune" (*Suite bergamasque*, 1890-1905). In the latter, during the final phrases before the coda, there is a bell-like, mid-piano accent and several measures of interval and chord patterns which resound when echoed in different octaves. These rudimentary sonorities forecast the recapitulation of "Reflets dans l'eau [Reflection in the Water]" (*Images*, 1905).

The guitar, like the bell, became a familiar evocation. Whereas the bell requires a legato touch, Debussy created the guitar not only through a staccato touch but also through picturesque Spanish elements of style. The examples which appear in both the early and very late work often utilize Spanish idioms without creating a Spanish atmosphere. Two songs, "Mandoline" (1880-83) and "Fantoches [Marionettes]" (*Fêtes galantes* [Elegant Holidays], 1892), evoke the eighteenth century world of Italian comedy. Many rolled chords appear in the piano accompaniment of "Mandoline" and momentarily evoke the guitar or bandurria when there are major ninths or intervals of the fourth of fifth in their sonority. The Aeolian mode and the Spanish vocalise contribute to the allusion. The chromatic piano introduction to "Fantoches" and the subsequent accompaniment only seem guitaresque with the appearance of Spanish elements in the composition (the Phrygian mode, the triplet pattern and the syllable "la" in the vocalise, etc.). The main theme of the piano work "Danse" (1890) has an accompaniment figure which utilizes the rolled chords that again simulate the guitar most clearly when the major ninth chord and intervals of the fourth, fifth or second are involved. The alternating fourths and fifths of the middle section are more definitive. By 1901, when Debussy wrote the two-piano work "Lindaraja" there is a growing element of maturity in his style as he began to create evocative atmospheres. "Lindaraja" was the first of six compositions in which Debussy clearly depicted Spain. The work begins with a simulation of the strum of the guitar--plucked fifths and seconds. Arpeggios terminate with chords--suddenly strummed fortissimo. An evocation of a *cante jondo* is accompanied by guitaresque pedals. However, the composition is still rudimentary and often seems to be a study for "La Soirée dans Grenade [Evening in Grenada]" (*Estampes*, 1903).

The Staccato Touch

The staccato touch was used by Debussy not just to evoke the guitar, but later as an adjunct to the movement of the faune, the cake walk of General Lavine, the roll of a drum. Staccato and portamento were also a part of Debussy's "mocquer" spirit.

A rapid staccato touch is possible on the piano because of the double escapement modification wherein the piano key can be restruck before it has returned to its original position. The modification also facilitates a rapid repetition of the same note; it facilitates trill patterns. In a prelude, "La Danse de Puck" (1909-10), trills are often sonorous vibrations which create atmosphere. An early example of this type of writing can be seen in the piano accompaniment to the song "Chevaux de Bois [Wooden Horses]" (*Ariettes oubliées* [Forgotten Airs], 1888). There are single trills and trills with the adjunct of a second or a chromatic bass line, all in one hand; the other hand has either the melody or staccato chords of accompaniment. The development of the second theme of the "Prélude" (*Pour le Piano*) has an accompaniment figure which is in essence a slow trill between pedal tones and forecasts the tremolos and murmurings that sustain atmospheric color in the later works. Less felicitous examples occur in the piano duet "March écossaise [Scotch March]" (1891) where ornamented trills are used to simulate the color of the bagpipe.

The Evasion of Fixed Pitch

Though Debussy's instrument had fixed pitch, he created the allusion of a more flexible mechanism when he wrote melodic lines which recall the *cante jondo* of Andalusian folk singers. Essentially an Oriental vocal style, the melody of the *cante jondo* usually moves within the interval of a sixth, with the voice gliding from note to note through a series of infinitesimal gradations, dividing notes into intervals smaller than a semitone. Usually there is an obsessive insistence on a single note which may be accompanied by appogiaturas. The return to the dominant is also characteristic of the style. Despite the obvious difficulties of notation, the development theme of "Lindaraja" with its chromaticisms is an early example. The passage is rhythmically complex, imitating the rubato of the vocal style.

Debussy obscured tonality by many means, almost none of which have direct recourse to the mechanism of the piano. However, the use of the second interval, when well-played, blurs the fixed interval pattern of the piano. In "Le Jet d'eau [Fountain]" *Cinq Poèmes de Charles Baudelaire* [Five Poems of Charles Baudelaire], (1887-89), the pattern of repeated seconds, usually in the treble of the piano accompaniment, sustains the words of Baudelaire, "Dans la cour le jet d'eau qui jase [In the Court, the Fountain Splashes]." The piano accompaniment of the song "Les Angelus" (1891) is often a primitive pedal motif of seconds under which Debussy indicated "pédale sourdine [muted pedal]." A similar pattern of sustained seconds occurs just before the recapitulation in the piano accompaniment of the song "Dans le jardin [In the Garden]" (1891). (example 3) Debussy appended seconds to the parallel fourths and fifths in "Sarabande" or arranged chordal series so that the interval of the second was the apparent color.

Example 3

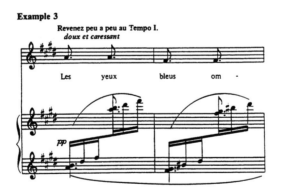

Debussy's use of the pentatonic scale obscured the mechanical construction of the piano. Few examples occur in the early work. The primary melodic pattern of "La Flûte de Pan" terminated in the pentatonic mode. The beginning of the piano phrase which introduces the song "En Sourdine [Muted]" (*Fêtes galantes*,

1891) is in the pentatonic mode. However, major examples don't occur until Debussy evoked Oriental atmospheres in his later compositions.

Sustained Sound: the Piano Pedal; Harmonic Pedals

Sustained sound was a requisite for creating atmosphere in the music of Debussy. A beautiful legato tone - the so-called transparent legato, requires striking the key with as little shock as possible, the arm and wrist supple, the fingers literally feeling into the keys to know exactly where the let-off, or escapement, begins, then sounding the note quickly but sustaining the touch until perfectly prepared to sound the next tone.

The sustaining pedal is an adjunct to the keyboard performance of Debussy's music. To "breathe" with it, as Debussy suggested, requires total flexibility to ease the pressure of the foot only slightly or completely, or to fluctuate the foot gently to aid in the creation of atmospheric movement.

As Debussy's style developed, he used the tonal range of his instrument in a virtuoso manner, attaching different sonorous values to musical patterns at different pitches which were sounded simultaneously. Sustained sound in such instances is impossible without the piano pedal. In the beginning, there are examples of sustained chords in the right hand, mid-piano--the left in the bass. Octave or interval patterns follow above and beyond the right hand chord and carry some of the tones from the chord. It is the piano pedal that sustains the initial chord sonority through the figuration. Examples appear in the piano accompaniment to the song "Paysage sentimental [Sentimental Landscape]" (1880-83), in the section just before the recapitulation and in "Danse" (1890). The middle section of "Danse" contains several measures of sustained chords with a more extended figuration area of repeated intervals. The passages in "Danse" forecast the sustained measures in the middle section of "Masques" (1904).

Debussy's extensive use of tones, intervals, chords or motifs as harmonic pedals is a method of sustaining sound and again requires the adjunct of the piano pedal. Countless examples abound even in the early work; several have already been mentioned. A very low A, singly or in octaves, underlies pages of "Prélude" (*Pour le piano*). Brief inner pedal motifs at the end of the song "Le Balcon" (*Cinq Poems de Charles Baudelaire*) forecast the inner movement in later works such as "La Cathédrale engloutie" (*Préludes,* 1909-10). The gliding of outer parts over stationary inner tones already appear in the chord structure of "Lindaraja." In essence, the rubato chords after the opening theme in the celebrated "Clair de lune" move in a similar manner over a bass pedal.

****

Until this point, the examples are important only because they foreshadow the work of a unique composer.

FOOTNOTES

1. *Lettres de Claude Debussy à son éditeur*, Paris, A. Durand et fils, 1927 Janvier, 1915.

    Before entering the Conservatoire, Debussy studied briefly with Madame Mauté de Fleurville who may have been a pupil of Chopin.

2. Ibid., 1er Septembre, 1915.

3. Ibid., 9 Octobre, 1915.

4. As early as 1881, the piano accompaniment to the song "Zéphyr" is composed of legato sequential passages in which wide-spread harmonic intervals are sustained by a bass pedal.

COMPOSITIONS CITED IN PART II*

Piano Solo

1890	Ballade (Slave).
	Danse.
	Valse romantique.
1890-05	*Suite bergamasque*: Clair de lune.
1892	Nocturne.
1884-1901	*Pour le piano*: Prélude, Sarabande, Toccata.
	The "Sarabande" appeared first in a supplément of *Le Grand Journal*, Février, 1896.
1904	Masques.
1904-05	*Images* (1re séries): Reflects dans l'eau, Hommage à Rameau, Mouvement.
	The second work was transcribed for piano duet by Debussy (Durand, 1905).
1907-08	*Images* (2e séries): Et la lune descend sur le temple qui fut.
1909-10	*Douze Préludes*, (1re livre): La Cathédrale engloutie.

1910-13	*Douze Préludes*, (2e livre): Feux d'artifice.

Piano Duet

1891	Marche écossaise sur un thème populaire (Marche des Anciens Comtes de Ross.)
	Orchestrated by Debussy in 1908 (Jobert, 1911).

Two Pianos

1901	Lindaraja.

Piano and Orchestra

1889-90	*Fantasie*.

36

Songs

1880-03	Mandoline (Poetry of Paul Verlaine).
1887-89	*Cinq Poèmes de Baudelaire*: Le Balcon, Le Jet d'eau.
	Le Jet d'eau was orchestrated by Debussy (Durand, 1907).
1888	*Ariettes Oubliées* (Poetry of Paul Verlaine): Chevaux de bois.
1891	*Deux Romances* (Poetry of Paul Bourget): Les Cloches.
	Les Angelus (Poetry of G. leRoy).
	Dans le Jardin (Poetry of Paul Gravollet).
	Fêtes galantes (Poetry of Paul Verlaine, 1re séries, 2e version): En sourdine, Fantoches.
1897-98	*Chansons de Bilitis* (Poetry of Pierre Louÿs): La Flûte de Pan.

* The entire collection of a work is not listed, only the individual compositions cited.

PART III

THE MATURE WORK

It is not until the appearance of *Estampes* [Prints] (1903) that one finds a semblance of a coherent style which reaches its fullest development in the *Préludes* (1909-13). Even the titles of the compositions signal the moment; a toccata becomes "Jardins sous la pluie," a suite, *Images*. The imagery that one associates with painting is enveloped with the atmospheric color of Debussy's particular compositional style. The tonal pictures shimmer with sparkling water, fireworks, dancing snow and cathedral bells. As the style matured, the elaborate pianism of "L'Isle joyeuse [Joyous Isle]" and "Reflets dans l'eau" became the tightly knit "Des Pas sur la neige [Steps in the Snow]" and "Minstrels," wherein the poetry is more concentrated, perhaps more poignant. Piano sonority was explored throughout the developed style. Earlier, the different elements were often seen separately. Now, one type of sonority supports another, for there is a splendid coherence in Debussy's mature style.

There is ample material for the piano virtuoso in this era. Earlier, purely pianistic passages existed, sometimes with quite difficult measures. However, the arpeggios, scale patterns, melodies supported by chords, etc., were often rudimentary displays of piano technique. Now, the pianistic passages project strong musical ideas that exploit the enormous range of sonority possible at the keyboard.

Traditional Pianistic Patterns Become Evocative

Scale passages become "Cloches à travers les feuilles" [Bells (heard) through the Leaves] (*Images*, 1907-08); a pattern of whole tones is first played portamento, with the first "bell" tone accented and sustained with the two piano pedals. Over the passage is the indication, "doucement sonore," [softly sonorous]. Then the pattern continues in the left hand while the right plays an ascending and descending whole-tone scale and the melodic motif which is an inversion of the first pattern. (example 4)

Example 4.

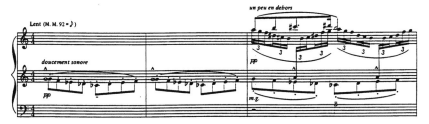

In the ironic "La Plus que lente" [More than 'La Valse Lente'--at that time a popular tune in Paris] (1910), mounting scale passages, which are a bridge between the first and second themes, are a parody of popular vamps.

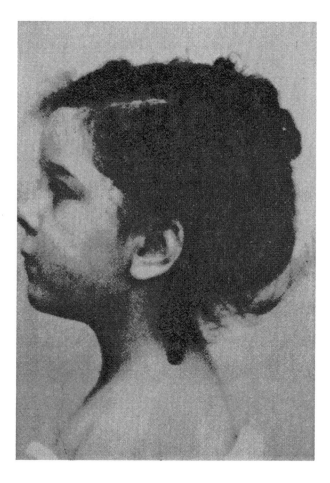

Chouchou (Claude-Emma) Debussy, 1911. Born October 30, 1905. Debussy's beloved daughter died a year after him because of a misdiagnosed illness. Debussy dedicated the *Children's Corner* to Chouchou "with a gentle apology for what is to follow."

The inspiration for "Poisson d'or" was a panel of Japanese lacquer owned by Debussy showing a goldfish and its reflection in the water. (Dolly de Tinan, stepdaughter of Debussy.)

Actually, few traditional scale passages exist. Since Debussy did not like to use his thumb, there are relatively few measures where the thumb must pass under the hand. Instead, there are countless examples of three- and four-note conjunct patterns which are interchanged between the hands, often in exotic sonorities. In "Doctor Gradus ad Parnassum" (*Children's Corner*, 1906-08), the gentle bridge passage after the first theme is an exchange of scale-like material rendered ambiguous by the omission of two notes. In the same suite, "The Snow is Dancing" is a miniature, though difficult toccata, in which the four fingers of the right hand sound portamento the four-note pattern which Debussy indicated should be played "doux et estompé" [soft and patterned]. The right hand then alternates, note for note with the left hand, the same pattern; then the thumb of the left hand must also sustain the melancholy melody. Flights of the pentatonic scale, with the hands alternating, animate "Voiles" [Veils or Sails]" (*Préludes*, 1909-10) in the climax before the recapitulation. "Mouvement" (*Images*, 1905) derives impetus from a rapid and repetitive three-note conjunct pattern played first in one hand then the other. The beginning three-note pattern of "Feux d'artifice" (*Préludes*, 1910-13) is an exploration of the piano as a two-keyboard instrument, the left hand on the white keys, the right on the black. The piano is a two-keyboard instrument during the primary theme of "Brouillards" [Fog] (*Préludes*, 1910-13), the right hand sounding the pentatonic scale, the left, the Mixolydian mode.

Arpeggios, too, are not just technical displays but suggest the sparkle of water or the movement of "Poissons d'or" [Goldfish] (*Images*, 1907-08). In this work, they often appear as flights of sound between sustained melody over which Debussy might indicate "capricieux et souple," as during the statement of the second theme. (example 5)

Example 5.

A rapid arpeggio passage moving from piano to forte enlivens "Brouillard" with a polytonal mixture, the pentatonic scale in one hand and an arbitrary Debussy pattern in the other. Before the recapitulation in the same work, arpeggios are steps on the black keys, intervals of the fourth and fifth over a melancholy theme, which for Debussy may have conveyed the movement of fog. Rapid arpeggio-scale mixtures in which there is a mingling of the pentatonic and whole-tone scales illuminate "Feux d'artifice." The west wind moves in arpeggios over bass pedals and forms a dramatic crescendo of alternating tonalities ('Ce qu'a vu le Vent d'Ouest" [What the West Wind Has Seen], (*Préludes*, 1909-10).

Usually, at this time in Debussy's work, it is not a question of an arpeggio or a scale but a passage of repetitive sound mingling conjunct and disjunct intervals to create atmospheric color. The virtuosity of "L'Isle joyeuse" (1904) depends on the pianist's ability to endure almost excessive repetition of pianistic figures. The recapitulation of "Jardins sous le pluie" [Gardens in the Rain] (*Estampes*) grows out of an arpeggio pattern, with omitted inner tones, sustained by a bass pedal of octaves over which Debussy indicated "mystérieux." The second theme of "Reflets dans l'eau" is stated in the left hand beneath a cascade of sound in the right hand--a scale-like grouping of the fingers on three consecutive black keys which must then pass over the thumb on C or C-flat. Debussy indicated "doux et expressif" over the passage which ranges widely in pitch. The recapitulation of the chorale of "La Cathédrale engloutie" [The Submerged Cathedral] (*Préludes*, 1909-10) is heard

"Les fées sont d'exquises danseuses...." A. Rackham's illustration for *Peter Pan in Kensington Gardens* (James Matthew Barrie, London, 1906). Both Chouchou and Debussy enjoyed the Barrie book. Hachette published the French translation in 1907. Debussy used the title for the fourth prelude in the second book of *Préludes*.

over a six-note repetitive bass pattern which when sustained by the two piano pedals, becomes "flottant et sourd" [floating and muffled].

The trill was a prodigious sonorous tool in Debussy's pianistic vocabulary. The ironic citation of the folk tune "Nous n'irons plus au bois" [We Will Not Go Anymore to the Woods] as the second theme of "Jardins sous la pluie" occurs over a slow inner pedal--in essence, a slow trill, to which is appended a chromatic line. In the accompaniment of the song "Crois mon conseil" [Believe Me] (*Le Promenoir des deux amants* [The Two Lovers' Promenade]) (1910), the pianist, in the recapitulation, must sustain a continuous soprano pedal--a trill, with the fourth and fifth fingers and held inner tones, while playing the melody in the left hand. As Debussy sought pianistic means to create atmosphere, the question of whether the rapid, alternating movement between notes was an interval of a second, third or fifth was inconsequential. The classic trill very often became a vibration, a tremolo. The shimmering and tonally ambiguous introduction which becomes the accompaniment for the first theme of "Poisson d'or" is a kind of trill. The giant arpeggios in the beginning of "Ce qu'a vu le Vent d'Ouest" subside to a mysterious bass tremolo. Puck ("La Danse de Puck") moves in a luminous atmosphere of repetitious interval patterns and skips over chromatic rumbles. Fairies (Les Fées sont d'exquises danseuses" [Fairies are the Exquisite Dancers], *Préludes*, 1910-13) dance in an atmosphere of tremolos and aerial high-pitched trills which become chromatic flights as they ascend. (example 6)

Example 6.

A trill as a means of prolonging sound in Debussy's work is inevitably sustained by the piano pedal and colored by harmonic pedals. Harmonic pedals whether as single tones, intervals, chords or motifs, became virtuoso colors in Debussy's composition at this time, for he explored simultaneously the great range of touch possible at the piano keyboard as well as the elements of pitch and dynamics.

Sustained Sound; Harmonic Pedals

Throughout this study, sustained tones have appeared in numerous examples. Their usage becomes more interesting in the developed style because of the manner in which Debussy used each to create atmospheric color. Jimbo, the elephant, is lulled by a motif from the children's folk tune "Do do l'enfant do" in the pentatonic mode over harmonic pedals, seconds with a very low bass under which Debussy indicated "les 2 [piano] pédales" (Jimbo's Lullaby," *Children's Corner*). The spirit of "Le Faune" (*Fêtes galantes*, 1904) is evoked in the song's piano introduction by a repeated rhythmic staccato bass pattern--a jig--over which is notated: "trés lointain, sans nuances, mais pourtant bien rythmé" [very far away, without nuances, nevertheless rhythmic]. "Des Pas sur la neige" (*Préludes*, 1909 -10) is a poignant study from the first sustained tones--a measured walk of seconds under which Debussy noted: "Ce rhythme doit avoir la valeur sonore d'un fond de paysage triste et glacé" [This rhythm must create the sonorous quality of a sad and frozen landscape].   (example 7)

Example 7.

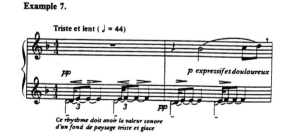

A gateway of the Alhambra Palace, Grenada. This postcard from Manuel de Falla inspired the creation of "La Puerta del Viño." (Dolly de Tinan, stepdaughter of Debussy.)

In "Feuilles mortes" [Dead Leaves] (*Préludes*, 1910-13), harmonic pedals at three pitch and dynamic levels all played with different piano touches lend chromatic support for the simple melodic line sounded mid-piano "un peu en dehors" [a little apart].   (example 8)

Example 8.

Except for brief interludes, a D-flat habanera pedal in the bass of "La Puerta del viño" [The Wine Gateway] (*Préludes*, 1910-13) establishes a Spanish atmosphere throughout the composition.   One of the composer's most effective works is "La Cathédrale engloutie."   The entire composition is supported by harmonic pedals. The beginning and primary motif moves between sustained treble and bass chords with the indication: "Profondémont calme [Very calm] ("Dans une brume doucement sonore" [In a soft sonorous mist]).   The notations throughout the composition indicate a preoccupation with sonorous and physical atmosphere whether the notation is "doux et fluide" [soft and fluid] over the bell-like first theme which revolves around an accented pedal tone, "peu a peu sortant de la brume" [little by little coming out of the fog] over the following developmental area wherein Debussy changed the tonal color and accompaniment pattern with each change of dynamics or "sonore sans dureté" [sonorous but not hard] over the parallel triads of the chorale, reminiscent of faux-bourdon, a fortissimo passage in which the doubling of sound must be rich but not too bright.

Rouen Cathedral, West Facade, Sunlight, 1894. Claude Monet (1840-1926). Though there is no evidence that Debussy knew Monet, he admired his work. *Photograph permission, the National Gallery of Art, Washington, D.C.*

The Exploration
of Orchestral Sonorities at the Keyboard

Debussy began exploring orchestral sonorities at the keyboard in his early work. At that time, the effect of bell tones was rudimentary. The evocation is prodigious in "La Cathédrale engloutie, " a composition in which there are few measures that cannot be explored by the pianist. Particularly effective are the many pedals sustained in the bass or treble while melodic patterns are repeated mid-piano. Debussy explored the singing quality of the instrument throughout the work. He used the resonating piano tone to create the characteristic dissonant clangor of bells. (example 9)

Example 9.

From the beginning accents of the whole-tone scale, the title of "Cloches à travers les feuilles" is suggestive. Bells resound throughout. Debussy's pianos probably had a long and ample range of higher harmonics. Therefore, it is not surprising that throughtout the mature work, bells resound in the lucid upper register of the instrument. Bell sounds are heard in the coda of "La Soirée dans Grenade" when a pianissimo habanera on a high C-octave rings over a recapitulation of the first theme. The clear treble octave on C rings early in "D'un cahier d'esquisses" [Sketchbook] (1903). Octaves which are to resound from the top note to the bottom as a bell-like arpeggio contribute to the sonorous color of the coda of "Reflets dans l'eau" over which Debussy noted: "Dans une sonorité harmonieuse et lointaine" [In a harmonious and faraway sonority].

Earlier, the Pandean pipe was noted in "La Flûte de Pan." The instrument is frequently evoked poetically in the piano duets *Six Epigraphes antiques* (1900-14). The title of the composition helps create the illusion. In the first, "Pour invoquer Pan, dieu du vent d'été" [To Evoke Pan, God of the Summer Wind], the rounded phrases and repetitious patterns of the primary theme in the pentatonic mode introduce the work. A flute-like instrument in "Pour la danseuse aux crotales" [For the Snake Dancer] is evoked by the treble of the piano, conjunct intervals and a rapid legato touch. The pan pipe appears in "Pour l'Egyptienne," wherein the style is more chromatic and repetitious. In the piano's introductory phrases to the song "Le Faune," Debussy signaled the instrumental evocation "ainsi qu'une flûte" [as a flute], then wrote a brief, sequential, scale-like passage colored by augmented seconds. In the prelude "Les Sons et les parfums tournent dans l'air du soir" [The Sounds and the Perfumes Turn in the Evening Air] (1909-10), Debussy indicated, "come une lointaine sonnerie de cors" [as a distant sounding of horns], then wrote a motif of parallel thirds and fourths, mid-piano, accented by very low- and high-pitched intervals. The pianist, feeling into the notes as Debussy might have done, allowing little movement of the fingers and hand, can eerily evoke a horn-like sound. (example 10)

Example 10.

Comme une lointaine sonnerie de Cors

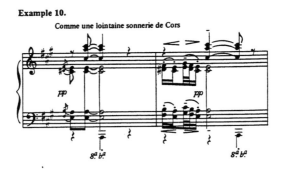

The cadence of a drum is unmistakable in "Minstrels" (*Préludes*, 1910-13). It is implied in the beginning of the climax of "L'Isle joyeuse, " when repetitious rhythmic dissonances are a bass pedal for the theme in the right hand, which also sustains an inner pedal with the forefingers of the hand.

The evocation of the guitar was noted in the early works with the best examples from "Lindaraja," a composition in which Debussy attempted to evoke a Spanish atmosphere. In the mature work, examples occur in piano compositions which evoke Spain: "Soirée dans Grenade" (*Estampes*, 1903), "La Sérénade interrompue" [The Interrupted Serenade] (*Préludes*, 1909-10) and "La Puerta del viño" (*Préludes*, 1910-13). However, the specific color of the guitar itself is often seen in compositions which do not suggest Spain (i.e. "L'Isle joyeuse " (1904), "Serenade for the Doll" (*Children's Corner*, 1906-08) and "Ballade des femmes de Paris" [Ballad of the Parisian Women] (*Trois Ballades de François Villon*, 1910). Whether the guitar is more recognizable in a composition impregnated with picturesque Spanish elements is a question.

Debussy interspersed song and dance with guitar interludes in "Soirée dans Grenade." He was particularly preoccupied with the guitar touch transposed to the piano.

Debussy introduced "La Sérénade interrompue" with six plucked notes and the indication, "quasi guitarra." The composition is reminiscent of the Exposition of 1889, which Debussy visited with Robert Godet, Raymond Bonheur and Paul Dukas.[1] Julien Tiersot described a scene which Debussy must have witnessed:

> ...What I heard the best that night was a dance by two small children while other children played the guitar, marking their steps: at a moment, a small voice was heard over the strumming of the guitars, clear, exact, a little nasal, singing a sort of melisma, oriental in character, without doubt, one of the malagueñas which are, I believe, the songs the most characteristic of Spain; then the voice died away. The guitars continued their monotonous rhythm, another voice took up the same song while another stopped. The dance stopped, without a final effect, almost without conclusion.[2]

The brief composition is a mosaic of fragmentary song accompanied by the guitar, and guitar and dance interludes which create the evanescent color of Spain. The guitar usually is evoked through a staccato or portamento piano touch. Sometimes crisp, rapid arpeggios allude to the strum of the instrument at the end of a phrase. The parts which are guitaresque are usually repetitive, rhythmically and harmonically.

A guitar passage occurs in "La Puerta del viño" soon after the appearance of the first theme. It is composed of sequential descents, a mingling of the six-tone scale, the D-flat habanera pedal and a rubato fragment of melody in the Phrygian mode. (example 11)

Example 11.

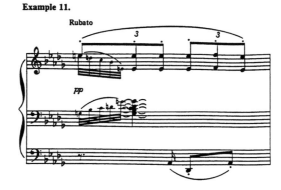

The evocation of the guitar can be elusive when portrayed on the piano without other picturesque elements that recall the instrument. The accompaniment for the primary theme of "L'Isle joyeuse is guitaresque both harmonically and in the use of the plucking and arpeggio technique. The primary theme of "Masques" evokes the guitar, or an element of the fantastic, in the repetitious alternation of the single note and fifths, which Debussy indicated should be "détaché et rythmé." In "Serenade for the Doll" *(Children's Corner),* performance of the theme requires that the pianist "pluck" the piano; the guitar appears throughout the composition, often as strummed--or plucked--seconds, thirds and fourths. In the recapitulation, the piano seems to become a guitar when chromatic chords must be strummed with taut fingers rather than rolled. (example 12)

Example 12.

Example 13.

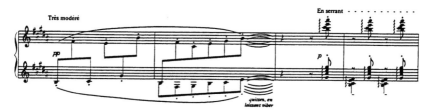

Example 14.

In Debussy's developed style, the color of a guitar often became more and more a very personal means of expression without the desire to create a Spanish atmosphere. Countless sonorous phrases involve guitar-like passages, both harmonically and in terms of an evocative touch, whether in the interludes of "Ballade des femmes de Paris" or in the introduction to "Les Collines d'Anacapri" [The Hills of Anacapri] (*Préludes*, 1909-10), when Debussy indicated after a portamento passage: "quittez, en laissant vibrer" [stop, but leave vibrating--lift the fingers, vibrate the pedal]. (example 13)

The gamelan is an orchestral effect in the compositions which purport to be Oriental. It is again in the pages of Julien Tiersot that one perceives something of the sound which Debussy must have heard in the exhibition from Java:

> From the ensemble of instruments came a very new sonority, one with charm; our percussion instruments are the most sonorous, the most vibrant, which our orchestras possess; those of the gamelan are, to the contrary, very soft, distinct, never disagreeable and perfectly musical.[3]

Two of Debussy's compositions recreate the Far East: "Pagodes" and "Et la lune descend sur le temple qui fut." The first composition, part of the piano suite (*Estampes*), is impregnated with what were, for Debussy, Oriental devices: duple meter with occasional ternary movement within the phrase; melodic lines that are gently suspended, rising toward the end and supported by major seconds; intervals of the fourth and fifth in parallel movement in the pentatonic mode; a miniature canon, etc. In the middle of the composition occurs a brief quasi-orchestral glimpse reminiscent of the eternal rhythmic repetitions which Debussy may have heard in the gamelan. The use of the pedals, the wide-spaced intervals and translucent movement in the left hand and the repetition are both Debussyian and Oriental. (example 14)

Sonorous Means Which Disguise
the Physical Construction of the Piano

Earlier Debussy's use of the pentatonic mode was mentioned as a sonorous means which disguised the physical construction of the piano. It is most effective when utilized in the oriental atmosphere of "Pagodes." (example 15)

Example 15.

It is often heard in "Et la lune descend sur le temple qui fut" (*Images*, 1907-08), a more poetic evocation of the Orient. One passage is reminiscent of the percussive intermingling of rhythms that Debussy may have heard at the Paris Exposition. (example 16)

Example 16.

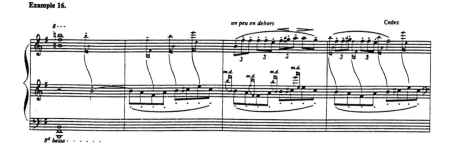

The ornamented octaves can sound bell-like. Debussy also utilized the lower register of the piano to evoke gongs in the composition.

The color of the pentatonic mode occurs in compositions which do not otherwise suggest the Orient. In "Jimbo's Lullaby" (*Children's Corner*), the lumbering walk of a toy elephant is evoked by a pianissimo bass theme in the pentatonic mode which Debussy indicated should be "doux et un peu gauche" [soft and a little awkward]. In "Serenade for the Doll," the guitaresque primary theme is in the pentatonic mode. "Feux d'artifice" is colored with the pentatonic mode. It is an exotic sonority used by Debussy to allude to the far-away, particularly in the recreations of the pan pipe in *Six Epigraphes antiques* .

In the early works, the use of the second interval also was noted as a way to evade the physical structure of the piano. The use of the major second was a part of Debussy's oriental palette. Batteries of seconds are part of the percussive movement in "Masques." The guitar which serenaded the doll ("Serenade for the Doll") was strummed in seconds. Seconds are a part of the rhythmic dissonance accompanying "Golliwogg's Cake Walk" (*Children's Corner*). They evoke the patter of rain in a polytonal toccata of seconds alternating with single notes in the composition "Pour remercier la pluie au matin" [To Offer Thanks for the Morning Rain] (*Six Epigraphes antiques*).

Earlier, it was noted that the recreation of a *cante jondo* ("deep song") expanded the seeming limitations of the piano because of the allusion to a song style rich in infinitesimal chromatic gradations. A good example occurs in "La Puerta del viño," when a suggestion of the fatalistic air is heard as the primary theme. It is written in the Hispano-Arabic mode, Rasdu-dh Dhil. There is the insistence on a single note with a sinuous repetition of notes revolving around it, a melismatic coloratura, rubato, long sustained notes followed by short triplets and rapid phrases, all over the habanera pedal. (example 17) One cannot reproduce at the piano infinitesimal gradations between tones which occur in a true *cante jondo*. Yet here there is such an ingenious use of the piano's physical resources in an evocation of a style that requires immense sensibility on the part of the pianist, a virtuoso's skill in the creation of a singing tone or the many gradations of tone possible in melismatic crescendos and descrescendos.

Example 17.

The Préludes : a Development
Toward an Economic Use of the Tools of Music

Traditionally, the pianist has thought of the piano as a singing instrument, capable of great fluidity of touch, a variety of tone, a great range in power and dynamics, exceeded by no other instrument and rarely equalled. At first, Claude Debussy composed within a predictable historic framework which he gradually expanded in his search for sonorous color. More and more as Debussy's style developed, he became preoccupied with atmospheric evocations and often with climatic conditions found at sea, in the fog, or at different times of day. The style was rich in harmonic innovations which permeated because of an enormous amount of repetition. Sounds were doubled, repeated sequentially and in parallel motion, heard again surrounded by the different accouterments of Debussy's style and supported by the fluctuations of the piano pedal. One is almost bombarded with sound in the repetitions of "L'Isle joyeuse" or "Masques." Gradually the repetition became less obvious in the myriad movements of a "Poissons d'or" or the multiple sonorities of "Cloche à travers les feuilles." The repetition became more interesting as the style developed. At the same time, the development was toward an economic use of the tools of music. Though there is some unevenness, many of the preludes became more succinct expressions of what had been attempted earlier. Within just a few measures are jewel-like colors, moments when the particular qualities of the piano are fully utilized for special sonorities. Many examples have already been noted.

The sonorities within a single composition can be prodigious; "Minstrels" (*Préludes*, 1909-10) requires almost every touch at the pianist's disposition. From the introductory march, which Debussy indicated should be "nerveux et avec humour," a music hall character is established. A battery of detached seconds alludes to the banjo. Accented parallel thirds accompanying a staccato motif recall the trumpet. The cadence of the drum is heard. The minstrel dances four measures; he sings a chromatic sustained melody another four measures; he jokes when Debussy indicated "moqueur" and wrote chromatic triads to be played portamento over a low marching bass. Moment by moment, the pianist must change his touch as the minstrel displays each talent. The pianist's fingers must sustain melody or capture the essence of a waltz in half a measure.

Two preludes describe the night: "Les Sons et les parfums tournent dans l'air du soir" (1909-10) and "La Terrasse des audiences du clair de lune" [The Terrace of Moonlight Audiences] (1910-13). Both works are episodic in nature, unified by the reappearance and transformations of a motif. The first is not only a microcosmos of Debussy's developed harmonic style, but also of his use of piano sonority. Color contrast is achieved pianistically through the alternation of legato and staccato motifs, quick changes in dynamics and the use of the full range of the piano for the simultaneous appearance of different melodic motifs often requiring different finger control. The entire composition of "La Terrasse des audiences du clair de lune" is notated on three staves. The range of the piano keyboard is used for sonorous effects, pitting touch against touch. (example 18) The last chords are especially effective if it is remembered that Debussy indicated that his chords should be played "moelleux"[4] [soft, velvety and not quite together].

Example 18.

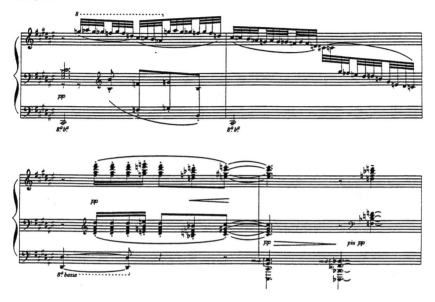

Much of the piano virtuosity in the works of Debussy is of a sublime poetic nature, requiring the perfection of individual tones, small motifs or a chordal phrase. Two preludes, however, allow some of the pyrotechnics so often popular. Even so, there is still a strong emphasis on sonorous color. The first, "Ce qu'a vu le Vent d'Ouest," is a study of a furious wind from the region of the Atlantic. It rolls up from the depths of the piano in giant and often tonally ambiguous arpeggios, scale patterns and chromatic chords. It subsides into tremolos that move menacingly in parallel motion. The only moment of peace in the composition is during an evocation of a patter of rain, which becomes a disturbing toccata of seconds punctuated with bright dissonances. The passage augments until the clash of the storm is heard as a fortissimo shriek of a pedal pattern in the treble, contrasting with the harsh doubling of seconds in the bass. Debussy indicated the character of the prelude when he wrote "angoisse." In contrast, "Feux d'artifice" (1910-13), animated and brilliant, depicts a gay juillet 14, especially with the brief citation of "La Marseillaise" at the end of the composition. Almost every pianistic technique is required of the performer. There are more conjunct passages than in the previous composition; many patterns use only a portion of the hand. The first motif is accompanied by a pattern played by the three middle fingers of each hand, one on the black keys, the other on the white, reminiscent of a two-keyboard instrument. Atmosphere is created not only by the choice of particular harmonies, but also by the use of the great fluidity of the piano to sound over and over a particular pattern as a sonorous background for a bright and accented motif.

The Legato Touch

The composer did not neglect the piano as a legato instrument. The songlike quality was used to evoke a particular atmosphere or a poetic idea. The primary melody of "La Fille aux cheveux de lin" [The Girl with the Flaxen Hair] (*Préludes*, 1909-10) recalls the poetic quality of the flute. Later in the work there occurs an excellent example of a translucent legato passage which requires not only finger dexterity but also the sure knowledge of where the key can be restruck before returning to the original position to create a gliding movement. (example 19)

Example 19.

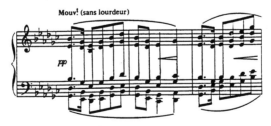

The themes of "The Little Shepherd" (*Children's Corner*) suggest the pastoral scene of a shepherd calling his sheep. The flute-like register of the piano, the modality, the fluent repetition and the calm mood suggest the berger's pipe. The movement of the sheep follows, signalled by a small jig recalling that the piano is also a rhythmic instrument.

The Staccato Touch

Debussy transformed the staccato touch as a technical term. Examples occur throughout the *Préludes*. A rhythmic staccato is part of the quick, crisp, slightly nervous walk of the "Minstrels" as they come onstage. It becomes a portamento to describe the movement of "General Lavine, eccentric." It is part of moments of irony and good humor in "Golliwogg's Cake Walk" (*Children's Corner*). A detached touch in the work of Debussy is frequently neither a crisp sound nor one that is sustained--neither staccata nor legato. Instead, it is a note or chord that is sounded, then sustained not by the fingers and hand but by the piano pedal. The resulting evanescent effect contributes to the evocation of bells of a submerged cathedral, the movement of fog or the nether world of an ancient ruin. (example 20)

Example 20.

The *Préludes* of Debussy are almost without exception compositions which recall elements from Debussy's world. They suggest the composer's interests--the English Music Hall, Shakespeare, Baudelaire, French legend, Spanish music, the antique world. The one exception, "Les Tierces alternées" [Alternated Thirds] (1910-13), is a study of thirds, a miniature toccata, which Debussy indicated should be played "doucement timbrées" [softly struck]. The problem for the pianist is one of gentle but firm fingers and a supple wrist.

FOOTNOTES

1.   Léon Vallas, *Debussy et son temps*, Paris, Alcan, 1932, pp. 80-93.

2.   Julien Tiersot, *Musiques pittoresques, promenades musicales à l'Exposition 1889*, Paris, Fischbacher, p. 71.

3.   Ibid., p. 33.

4.   Oswald d'Estrade-Guerra, a pupil of Ricardo Viñes, the pianist who introduced many of Debussy's works, related Viñes instructions in this regard.

COMPOSITIONS CITED IN PART III

Piano Solo

1903   D'un cahier d'esquisses.

Estampes: Pagodes, Soirée dans Grenade, Jardins sous la pluie.

Jardins sous la pluie first appeared as an exercise in an early *Images* for piano (1894).

1904   L'Isle joyeuse.

Transcribed for orchestra by B. Molinari after the indications of Debussy (Durand, 1923).

Masques.

1904-05   *Images* (1re séries): Reflets dans l'eau, Mouvement.

1906-08   *Children's Corner*: Doctor Gradus ad Parnassum, Jimbo's lullaby, Serenade for the Doll, The Snow is Dancing, The Little Shepherd, Golliwogg's Cake Walk.

1907-08   *Images* (2e séries): Cloches à travers les feuilles, Et la lune descend sur le temple qui fut, Poissons d'or.

1909-10	*Préludes* (1re livre): Voiles, Les sons et les parfums tournent dans l'air du soir, Les Collines d'Anacapri, Des Pas sur la neige, Ce qu'a vu le Vent d'Ouest, La Fille aux cheveux de lin, La Sérénade interrompue, La Cathédrale engloutie, La Danse de Puck, Minstrels.
	Debussy transcribed Minstrels for Violin and Piano (Durand, 1910).
1910	La Plus que lente.
1910-13	*Préludes* (2e livre): Brouillards, Feuilles mortes, La Puerta del viño, Les Fées sont d'exquises danseuses, Général Lavine--eccentric, La Terrasse des audiences du clair de lune, Les Tierces alternées, Feux d'artifice.

Piano Duet or Two Pianos

| 1900-14 | *Six Epigraphes antiques:* Pour invoquer Pan, dieu du vent d'été, Pour la danseuse aux crotales, Pour l'Egyptienne, Pour remercier la pluie au matin. |
| | This work began as *musique de scène* for the *Chansons de Bilitis* of Pierre Louÿs, 1900-01. |

Songs

1897-99	*Chansons de Bilitis* (The Poetry of Pierre Louÿs): La Flûte de Pan.
1904	*Fêtes galantes* (2e séries): (The poetry of Paul Verlaine): Le Faune.
1910	*Le Promenoir des deux amants* (The poetry of Tristan Lhermite): Crois mon conseil, chère Climène.
	Trois Ballades de François Villon: Ballade des femmes de Paris.
	Orchestrated by Debussy (Durand, 1911).

PART IV

THE LAST YEARS

The Twelve Etudes

In 1915, Debussy was to devote himself to a series of *Douze Etudes* which he dedicated to "the memory of Frederic Chopin" and remarked to his editor:

> The six "Etudes" which remain are finished; there is only a question of copying. I am content to have finished a work which, without false vanity, can take a particular place. In regard to the technique of the "Etudes," they will usefully prepare pianists to understand better that one can't enter into music with questionable hands![1]

Debussy made several remarks, unorthodox for his time, in the preface of the work:

> Intentionally, the present *Etudes* don't contain any fingering and here is the reason: A fingering cannot be adapted logically to different conformations of the hand. Modern pianism thought to have resolved this question by superimposing many fingerings, which is only an embarrassment...Music then takes on the aspect of a strange work or an unexplainable phenomena; the number of fingers would have to be increased...
>
> The absence of fingering is an excellent exercise which prevents a spirit of contradiction and verifies these eternal words: "one is never better served than by oneself."

The twelve *Etudes* of Debussy evolved technically from the Chopin he admired. Each composer concerned himself with basic pianistic technique which he sublimated to elements of musical style. What previously had been a search for atmosphere in Debussy became a more dramatic and percussive personal expression which still involved the special sonority of the piano. In Debussy's last works, there are measures creating atmospheric color. However, those devices which were often used earlier to evoke the atmosphere of Spain, the English Music Hall, etc., became a part of a more personal declamation in which one is often aware of Debussy's anguish over the war, his terminal illness and an inevitable stylistic change that was part of the general movement of music history away from the nineteenth century.

Like Chopin, Debussy was concerned with studies for the five fingers and their movement, individually or ensemble, studies for the wrist, for the use of the arm (i.e. "Pour le cinq doigts,) [For the Five Fingers]," "Pour les tierces [For the Thirds]," "Pour les degrés chromatiques [For the Chromatic Tones]," etc.). Unlike Chopin, he included a special study of theory and of sonority (i.e. "Pour les agréments [For the Ornaments]," "Pour les sonorités opposées [For the Opposed Sonorities].") There is always an element of humor in Debussy's work. The titles of the tenth and eleventh etudes are "Pour les sonorités opposées" and "Pour les arpèges composés [For the Composed Arpeggios]." The full title of the first etude is: "Pour le 'cinq doigts' d'après Monsieur Czerny [For the Five Fingers after M. Czerny]." Debussy recalled innumerable Czerny habits. He appended whimsical dissonances and amusing motifs to traditional patterns. He rhythmically altered five-finger motifs and colored an entire composition with constant dynamic shadings. An amusing footnote is included with the study "Pour le huit doigts [For the Eight Fingers]." Since Debussy, the pianist, did not like to use his thumb, he said:

> In this etude, the changing position of the hands makes the usage of the thumbs inconvenient; the performance would become acrobatic.

Because of the percussive nature of the etudes and the preoccupation with harmonic and rhythmic change, there is not too much occasion for extensive periods of atmospheric color which were seen earlier. When the passages do occur, usually there is an extended period of rhythmic repetition and often a chromatic and sequential build-up of a particular motif with an augmentation of the tempo and dynamics. There is a greater harmonic sophistication and a greater simplicity of style in which nonessentials are eliminated. There is an economy of means now in such examples as the primary theme and its development in the etude "Pour les accords [For the Chords]" or the second section of "Pour les octaves [For the Octaves]" as opposed to the extended repetitions earlier in "L'Isle joyeuse" or the awkward transitions in "Mouvement." This economy of means was noted in such preludes as "Minstrels." It is a stylistic tendency which also prevails in the songs of the period around 1910.

In Chopin's *Etudes*, song is always present and the pianist frequently uses a legato touch or a firm portamento. The modern pianist often changes his tone color to denote changes in Chopin's harmony. A basic problem in the performance of the Debussy *Etudes* is the need to create a cohesive style despite the constant harmonic change and the extended sonorous palette available. Too much diversity can create a lack of unity. Fortunately, a repetition of rhythmic and melodic patterns and dynamic development unify what could be fragmented compositions. Earlier, Debussy used sonority to sustain poetic ideas, particular atmospheric colors. Now, the different sonorous elements have been assimilated and have become part of a personal, sometimes abstract, statement.

The etude "Pour les sonorités opposées" is interesting because it encompasses so many of the ideas discussed earlier though now presented under the guise of technique. Patterns appear which are Chopinesque, especially when Debussy used sustained melody and detached chromatic accompaniment in the same hand. Debussy, more than Chopin, utilized the bass and treble of the piano for sonorous bell-like harmonic pedals with a melodic movement of inner voices. At times, there is the ethereal quality found in descriptive moments in the *Préludes* ; only now, the examples are no longer picturesques but abstract presentations of sound.

Various military motifs are apparent in Debussy's last work. Debussy lamented World War I, felt a renewed patriotism and often used military motifs as a symbol of heroism. The motif which introduces the second section of the etude, though more complicated melodically than the usual military calls, does seem a poetic evocation because of the repetitive internal pattern and the accents. (example 21).

Example 21

Throughout the etude, accompanying each appearance of this motif are numerous indications for every kind of dynamic touch: "de plus près [closer]" when the motif appears over a chain of chords which are marked "sempre calando [always diminishing];" "de loin [far away] " when the motif is abbreviated and marked pianissimo and staccato, then "de plus loin [farther away]" in the final statement an apparent retreating of the military.

The cadence of drums and the sonority of horns appear occasionally throughout the section further identifying a military atmosphere.

Similar motifs appear in other works of the period, for example in the "Berceuse héroïque" (1914) which was dedicated to Albert I of Belgium and his soldiers in an evocation of trumpets in the distance. The rhythm, interval patterns and repetition evoke the military with the change of register and key and the Debussy indication "un peu en dehors." (example 22)[2]

Example 22

The etude "Pour les agréments" is harmonically somewhat less rich than the etude "Pour les sonorités opposées." However, Debussy was ingenious in his use of every kind of ornament. He abstractly used the ambiguous arpeggios which he once used to evoke the movement of the west wind. He used the tremolo type of background, which formerly would have accompanied the dance of Puck or the movement of fairies, to accompany a non-programmed sprightly theme. The guitar no longer accompanies a *cante jondo* or a nursery doll but a bass theme. The work abounds with a grotesque spacing of parts, sonorous bass pedals and every kind of legato and staccato touch. It is almost a pianistic *tour de force* every two measures.

The performance of the etude "Pour les notes répétées [For the Repeated Notes]" depends essentially on a fluid facility made possible by the double escapement mechanism of the modern piano. A toccata, which usually requires a staccato or a portamento touch, it can exact a finger staccato or a bravura detached touch requiring the full weight of the arm. Variety is the essence and can be intense.

En blanc et noir
Sonate pour violoncelle et piano
Sonate pour violon et piano

Essentially, the two-piano work, *En blanc et noir*, [In Black and White] (1915), the *Sonate pour violoncelle et piano* (1915) and the *Sonate pour violon et piano* (1916) mirror similar characteristics. All have pianistic passages that are reminiscent of earlier writing. The two-piano work begins with a type of broken chord with an accented tone found in "Dr. Gradus ad Parnassum" (*Children's Corner.*). The third section reflects passages from the *Six Epigraphes antiques* and "L'Isle joyeuse"--a catalogue of pianistic patterns that Debussy used throughout his life.

An assimilative guitaresque passage serves as an introduction to the Finale of the Sonata for Cello and Piano. (example 23)

Example 23

All three works have memorable sonorous moments often utilizing effects named earlier. The citation of "Ein' Feste Burg ist Unser Gott [A Mighty Fortress is Our God]" in the second portion of *En blanc et noir* provides a heroic moment in a work dedicated to "Lieutenant Jacques Charlot tué à l'ennemi en 1915, le 3 mars [Lieutenant Jacques Charlot killed by the enemy, March 3, 1915]." The theme is played with a firm legato in the right hand supported by a detached bass which Debussy indicated should be "poco marcato." A second piano provides strong rhythmic accents.

The second section of the work has more areas of sonorous color. It is introduced by military motifs and the plaintive notes of a Scotch jig which is over a G-sharp pedal--perhaps evocative of the bagpiper. There are the ornaments which one associates with the pipe and terraced dynamics, forte to pianissimo, as the march recedes.

Though the toccata finale is often like Ravel and reminiscent of the etude "Pour les notes répétées," Debussy utilized the rapid touch and brilliant sonority of the instrument. At one moment, an assimilation of a Spanish melisma occurs as a counterpoint to the toccata. (example 24)

Example 24

The second movements of both sonatas reflect Debussy's interest in the eighteenth century: a "Sérénade" in the cello sonata and an "Intermède" in the violin sonata. The "Intermède" has some of the most sonorous pianistic passages in the two works. The spirit of the *Fêtes Galantes* followed Debussy all of his life and appears as a motif in a brief scherzando section soon after the beginning. (example 25)

Example 25

Soon there is a forte piano passage with the gliding pedal effect first noted in "Clair de lune" and a pitting of chromatic piano sonority against the accents of the violin. (example 26)

Example 26

75

Another piano and violin passage follows with sonorous instrumental doubling against an inner pedal. (example 27)

Example 27

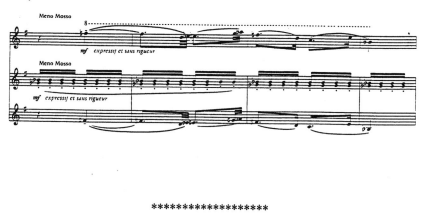

****

Despite the changes which occur in Debussy's last work and the immaturity of his early compositions, Debussy prodigiously utilized the sonorous resources of the piano. Though he never realized his first goal of being a concert artist, he knew all of the technical possibilities available to a skilled pianist. In the early work he often used the piano in traditional patterns. Until the very end, Debussy remembered the many roles of his instrument and wrote exquisite melodies, scintillating toccatas, sweeping cadenzas. However, in his full development, he uniquely employed the piano's sonorous resources as a painter of atmospheric scenes to evoke the plucking of a guitar, the dissonance of cathedral bells, a goldfish in bright waters or a toccata of raindrops.

This study has been an attempt to discuss only those elements in Debussy's work that could be directly associated with the qualities of a particular instrument and what they would inspire. Undoubtedly, the composer knew a modern piano, but he must have known one more translucent than contemporary models, one somewhat deficient in low harmonics, but able to produce a long and ample range of higher harmonics. This instrument may have inspired the pursuit of legato tones, the bell-like sonorities. Ultimately, it was the musician himself who was a poet of tone. Berthe Bert,[3] who knew the mature composer, remembered him seated for periods of time at his upright piano, experimenting with sound as a painter would explore values. Earlier, but similar, portraits were sketched by friends and fellow students at the Conservatoire. Finally, one recalls the remark of André Suarès:

> The play of Debussy was an incantation, the most immaterial music, with the greatest nuances one has ever heard. He didn't realize sonority as a pianist, never as a musician, but as a poet.

Debussy used the word "sonority" in its fullest sense. He understood the traditional definition of a resounding or vibrating tone; he indicated in his score "faites vibrer [vibrate]." However, since Debussy was concerned with atmospheric effects and sensual color, the interpretation was not expected to be orthodox. The pianist must lift his hands from the keyboard--as indicated by the simultaneous markings of a staccato touch and a sustained tone--and allow the tone to become part of an evanescent atmoshphere by fluctuating the piano pedal. The performance of Debussy's music requires not only finger dexterity, but the sure knowledge of where the key can be restruck before returning to the original position so that the tones will not be shocking. The problem, too, for the pianist is also often one of gentle but firm fingers with a supple wrist.

Debussy concentrated on so many sonorous effects that he required a prodigious use of the piano's resonating qualities. To explore the composer's work fully, a unique freedom is required of the pianist himself; for he cannot recreate the myriad   tones of a cathedral's bells or sustain adequately with his foot pedal the innumerable harmonic pedals without intense personal research. Just as the study of Debussy's harmony can be a preparation for the innovations of the twentieth century, a study of his resonant piano works can equip the instrumentalist today for exploration at his instrument.

FOOTNOTES

1.   *Lettres de Claude Debussy à son éditeur*, 27 Setptembre, 1915.

2.   The evocations in the two-piano work *En blanc et noir* (1915) are not definitive but do recall the military. They occur in the second of the three pieces which Debussy introduced with the François Villon "Ballade contre les ennemis de la France."

3.   Friend of the composer and former professor at the Ecole Normale de Musique, Paris.

COMPOSITIONS CITED IN PART IV

Piano Solo

1890-1905   *Suite bergamasque*: Clair de lune.

1904   L'Isle joyeuse.

1906   *Children's Corner*: Dr. Gradus ad Parnassum.

1914   Berceuse Héroïque pour rendre hommage à S. M. le
                     Roi Albert I de Belgique et à ses soldats.

                     Debussy orchestrated, 1914, (Durand, 1915).

1915   *Douze Etudes* (Livre I): Pour "les cinq" doigts
                     d'après Monsieur Czerny, Pour les tierces, Pour les
                     octaves, Pour les huit doigts.

                     Douze Etudes (Livre II): Pour les degrés
                     chromatiques, Pour les agréments, Pour les notes
                     répétées, Pour les sonorités opposées, Pour les
                     arpèges, Pour les accords.

Piano Duet

1900-14   *Six Epigraphes antiques.*

Two Pianos

1915   *En blanc et noir.*

Chamber Works

1915   *Sonate pour violoncelle et piano.*

1916-17   *Sonate pour violon et piano.*

STUDIES IN THE HISTORY AND INTERPRETATION OF MUSIC